*Mercier Press is the oldest independent Irish
publishing house and has published books in the
fields of history, literature, folklore, music, art,
humour, drama, politics, current affairs, law
and religion. It was founded in 1944 by John
and Mary Feehan.*

*In the building up of a country
few needs are as great as that of a publishing
house which would make the people proud of
their past, and proud of themselves as a people
capable of inspiring and supporting a world of
books which was their very own. Mercier Press
has tried to be that publishing house. On the
occasion of our fiftieth anniversary we thank
the many writers and readers who have
supported us and contributed to our success.*

*We face our second half-century
with confidence.*

IRISH
BISTRO COOKING

MICHAEL CLIFFORD

MERCIER PRESS

Mercier Press
PO Box 5, 5 French Church Street, Cork
16 Hume Street, Dublin 2

© Michael Clifford

A CIP for this book is available from the British Library

ISBN 1 85635 107 6

10 9 8 7 6 5 4 3 2 1

DEDICATION

To my wife Deirdre, our children Peter and Laura
To Paddy, Myread and family for all their kindness
And a big thank you to all our customers who have
supported us over the years

Printed in Ireland by Colour Books Ltd.

Contents

Introduction

Michael's Bistro happened when the property next door to Cliffords Restaurant became available. Should we or shouldn't we go ahead and try a concept of food completely different from what we were doing? Experience has shown that we have moved in the right direction.

There are days and evenings when you want – when you have to have – 'grand cooking'. But there are times when you want the simple kind. And these days, money and time enter into most people's calculations.

It's Cliffords for the gourmet dinner and the long lingering lunch – the Bistro is the mini gourmet with sharply focused food in a light, modern idiom, making extensive use of the same ingredients as the main restaurant but in a simple style.

Our Bistro is a small, chic, intimate space where people can feel at ease with their friends, and eat something delicious that does not demand much time or money.

Try out the recipes in this book and come to the Bistro, where there will be a warm welcome.

Eventually our style of food may be your home cooking.

Michael Clifford

SOUPS AND SAUCES

Parsnip and Garlic Soup

yields 1.5 litres

Ingredients

400g parsnips
30g butter
1 medium onion
6 cloves of garlic
1 tablespoon fresh thyme leaves
1 litre of chicken stock
250ml cream
1 bunch of tied herbs
Salt & milled black pepper to taste

Method: wash, peel and slice the parsnips. Peel and chop the garlic and onion. Place the parsnip, thyme, garlic and onion in a saucepan with the knob of butter. Sweat until the vegetables are soft. Add the chicken stock and the bunch of tied herbs and simmer for 15 to 20 minutes. Liquidise and pass through a fine sieve, add the cream and seasoning and correct consistency.

Homemade Chicken Soup with Lentils and Pearl Barley

yields 1.5 litres

Ingredients

**Knob of butter
200g lentils (pre soaked)
1 medium onion (sliced)
1.25 litres of good flavoured chicken stock
1 clove of garlic (crushed)
200ml cream
50g pearl barley (pre soaked)
1 bunch of tied herbs
1 stick of celery (chopped)
Seasoning to taste**

Method: rinse pearl barley and lentils under cold running water and reserve some lentils and barley for garnish. Cook them separately. Sweat onions, garlic and celery in a knob of butter and add lentils, pearl barley, chicken stock and bunch of tied herbs. Bring to the boil, skim well and then simmer for 30 minutes. Liquidise and pass through a sieve. Return to the boil, add cream and correct seasoning. Add garnish and serve.

Note: it is important to note that lentils and pearl barley mush be washed well. This is a hearty soup which would be ideal to serve on a cold winter's evening.

Michael's Nettle Soup

Ingredients

75g nettle leaves (blanched and chopped)
1 knob of butter
1 large onion
2 medium sized potatoes (peeled and washed)
$^1/_2$ clove of chopped garlic
1 bunch of tied herbs
1 leek (washed and chopped)
1.25 litres good flavoured chicken stock
250ml cream
Seasoning to taste

For Garnishing

50ml lightly whipped cream flavoured with $^1/_2$ teaspoon of Irish whiskey

Method: sweat onions, leek and garlic in a knob of butter and add nettles, potatoes and chicken stock with the bunch of tied herbs. Simmer for 15 to 20 minutes. Remove tied herbs and then liquidise and pass through a fine sieve. Add cream and return to the boil. Correct seasoning and consistency. Place a spoon of whiskey cream on each serving.

Note: this soup is ideally served with brown soda bread.

Cabbage and Smoked Bacon Soup

yields 1.5 litres

Ingredients

1 medium sized head of cabbage
2 medium sized potatoes (peeled and diced)
6 rashers of smoked bacon (chopped)
2 small onions (chopped)
1.5 litres of chicken stock
250ml fresh cream
Bunch of tied herbs
Seasoning to taste
30g butter

Method: wash and chop cabbage. Sweat the onion, cabbage and bacon in the butter for 3 minutes over gentle heat. Add the potato and chicken stock. Bring to the boil and skim. Add the herbs and cook for 20 minutes, simmering. Remove herbs.

Liquidise, and pass through a fine sieve. Add cream and return to the boil. Skim if necessary. Correct seasoning and consistency.

Michael's Bread Sauce

Ingredients

500ml milk
200g white breadcrumbs
50g butter
100ml cream
1 shallot (very finely diced)
$1/2$ teaspoon mixed spice
Salt & milled black pepper

Method: melt the butter in a saucepan, add the shallot and cook until soft, without colouring. Add the mixed spice, milk and cream and bring to the boil. Stir in the breadcrumbs. Season to taste and place in a sauce-boat until ready to serve.

Note: this is a variation of the old favourite bread sauce and goes well with poultry. The flavour may be enhanced and the consistency adjusted by adding the natural cooking juices from any roast.

Vinaigrette Dressing

yields ¹/₂ litre

Ingredients

125ml white wine vinegar
125ml virgin olive oil
125ml hazelnut oil
125ml vegetable oil
1 teaspoon of lemon juice
1 sprig of fresh thyme and rosemary
1 clove of garlic
12 white peppercorns
1 teaspoon of sea salt

Method: put herbs, garlic, salt and pepper into a storage jar. Combine all the liquids and pour into the jar.

Note: it is important to use good quality oils and vinegars to get the best results. Shake the jar well before serving.

STARTERS

Steamed Mussels and Clams Scented with Lemon Grass

serves 6

Ingredients

1.5kg mussels
1kg clams
1 lemon (sliced)
$1/2$ onion (diced)
1 bunch parsley
1 stick lemon grass
1 bay leaf
50ml white wine
50ml water
100ml cream
25g Beurre Manié
Seasoning to taste

Method: wash the mussels and clams well, ensuring to remove beards from the mussels. Chop the parsley leaves and reserve the stalks for cooking.

Place all of the ingredients except the cream, chopped parsley and Beurre Manié into a large pot. Steam for 4 to 5 minutes, until the shells are just open. Remove the shellfish and place into a serving dish.

Pass the cooking juices through a fine sieve into a small saucepan. Boil and add the cream. Boil again and whisk in the Beurre Manié. Add the chopped parsley and correct seasoning. Pour the sauce over the fish, serve immediately.

Note: lemon grass is now widely available and compliments fish dishes very well. However, if you wish to substitute lemon grass you can always use chopped root ginger.

A Stew of Clonakilty Black Pudding with Flageolet Beans and Homemade Sausages

serves 6

Ingredients

300g flageolet beans
1.5 litres chicken stock
25g lardons of smoked bacon
200g tin of plum tomatoes
1 tablespoon tomato purée
1 glass white wine
1 medium onion (diced)
2 cloves of garlic (crushed)
1 bunch of tied herbs
1 knob of butter
1 ring of Clonakilty black pudding (sliced)
6 homemade sausages
Salt & milled pepper to taste

Method: soak the flageolet beans for 4 hours in advance. Wash very well before use. Sweat onions and garlic in a knob of butter. Add the bacon, tomato purée and flageolet beans, then add the chicken stock, herbs, wine and tomatoes. Bring to the boil and simmer for 1 1/2 hours or until the beans are cooked, simmering constantly.

Fry the black pudding and sausages in a separate pan. Pour the bean stew into the serving dish and place the black pudding and sausages on top. Garnish with chopped, fresh herbs.

Avocado Filled with Fresh Crab and Bulb Fennel

serves 2

Ingredients

1 ripe avocado
25g bulb fennel
150g cooked crab meat
$^1/_2$ eating apple
50ml of lightly whipped cream
Juice of $^1/_2$ lemon
Salt & milled black pepper

Method: grate the apple and fennel, and combine with the crab meat and finely diced avocado. Add the whipped cream and lemon juice and season to taste. Serve in a bowl or avocado shell.

Note: this is best served in the summer as crab is in season.

Shrimp and Avocado Salad with a Warm Sherry Vinegar Dressing

serves 4

Ingredients

500g fresh shrimps (peeled)
Knob of butter
1 ripe avocado
1 bowl of assorted salad leaves to serve 4 persons
Vinaigrette dressing (see page 17)
1 tablespoon of sherry vinegar
1 tablespoon dry sherry
50ml olive oil
150ml sunflower oil
1 egg yolk
1 teaspoon Dijon mustard
1 teaspoon lemon juice
Salt & black milled pepper to taste

Method: peel and dice the avocado. Season the salad leaves and toss with avocado in a small amount of vinaigrette. Season the shrimps and fry them in a little butter, and then set aside.

Place the sherry and the sherry vinegar with the egg yolk in a small saucepan, place over a gentle heat and whisk constantly to form a sabayon. Remove from the heat, whisk in the mustard and gradually add the olive and sunflower oils. Add the lemon juice and season to taste. Arrange the salad leaves on a serving dish and place the shrimps around. Serve the warm dressing separately in a sauce boat.

Rillette of Duck and Pork

Ingredients

1.5kg duck legs
400g duck fat
1kg pork fat
350g pork fillet
1 whole carrot
1 small onion
2 cloves of garlic
Bunch of tied herbs
1 tablespoon sea salt
1 bottle of white wine
10g green peppercorns (crushed)
150ml water

Method: place the duck and pork fat into a deep roasting pan with the water. Melt fats in a moderate oven. Pass through a sieve into a clean roasting pan. Cool until luke warm and add remaining ingredients. Simmer for 1 hour. Drain off the fat and remove the herbs and vegetables. Remove the bones from the duck legs and flake into fine pieces. Do likewise with the pork fillet. Mix together and place in an Earthenware or Pyrex dish and pour on the cooking liquid. Store in fridge and use as required.

Note: ensure that all bones are removed as stated in the method. This is ideally served with toast and can be served as a starter or as an appetiser with drinks.

A Sauté of Lambs' Kidneys and Sweetbreads with a Cômpote of Tomatoes and Aubergines

Ingredients

2 lambs kidneys
100g lambs sweetbreads
$1/4$ aubergine (diced)
4 tomatoes (peeled, de-seeded and diced)
$1/2$ clove of garlic (crushed)
1 tablespoon of chopped chives
Seasoning to taste
Olive oil for cooking

Method: wash and blanch sweetbreads. Prepare by removing any excess fat or gristle and chop into pieces. Half the kidneys and remove outer skin. Also chop into pieces.

In a large frying pan, heat some oil and fry aubergine, tomato and garlic until soft. Season to taste and add chopped chives. Set aside. Wipe pan clean with kitchen towel, add some oil and heat until very hot. Add kidneys and toss quickly, then add sweetbreads and cook. Place kidneys and sweetbreads in the centre of a large serving dish. Then add aubergine and tomato mixture on top of kidneys and sweetbreads.

Serve immediately.

Tripe and Onion Soufflé

Ingredients

200g tripe
500ml milk
15g Beurre Manié
1 tablespoon of chopped parsley
1 egg yolk
2 tablespoons grated Cheddar cheese
$^1/_2$ medium sized onion
Whites of 4 eggs
Salt & milled black pepper

Method: wash tripe and cut into small cubes. Place tripe in a saucepan with onion and milk. Simmer for 45 minutes. Drain milk into a separate saucepan, bring to the boil and whisk in Beurre Manié and season to taste. Cool slightly and stir in egg yolk. Whisk egg whites with a pinch of salt until stiff and fold gently into sauce mixture. Butter a large soufflé dish and half fill with soufflé mixture. Then, in the centre, add tripe and onion and cover with remaining mixture. Sprinkle with Cheddar cheese and parsley. Cook in a moderate oven at 165°C for 13 minutes approximately. (During the cooking period, it is advisable to loosen the sides of the dish and continue to cook until ready). Serve immediately.

Stuffed Onions with Spicy Mince

serves 4

Ingredients

4 medium sized onions
100g minced beef
25g cooked kidney beans
Pinch of chilli powder
1/2 clove of garlic (chopped)
1 bunch of tied herbs
50ml tomato juice
200ml beef stock
Knob of butter
Salt and milled black pepper

Method: peel the onions, then blanch them for ten minutes. Remove centres and chop finely for the mince filling.

Filling: fry the onion, garlic and minced beef in a hot pan with a knob of butter. Add the chilli powder, kidney beans and tomato juice. Cook for five minutes (approximately). Place the filling into the centre of each onion, then braise in a small casserole dish, in the oven, by adding the beef stock and bunch of tied herbs. Cook for one hour (approximately). Correct seasoning and serve.

Note: a sauce can be made from the cooking juices and can be served over the onions if so desired.

Salad of Smoked Mackerel with Smoked Trout Mousse

serves 4

Ingredients

2 fillets of smoked mackerel
2 fillets of smoked trout
Selection of salad leaves
Vinaigrette (see page 17)
100ml natural yoghurt
100ml fresh cream
Lemon juice
Pinch of cayenne pepper
Salt & milled pepper to taste

Method: ensure that mackerel and smoked trout are free from skin and bones. Flake smoked mackerel into small pieces and set aside. Place smoked trout fillet into a food processor, add cream, purée and remove from food processor. Place in a bowl and fold in yoghurt. Add lemon juice and seasoning.

To Assemble Dish: toss salad leaves in vinaigrette. Place salad leaves in centre of a dish. Arrange mackerel neatly around salad. With two teaspoons, form smoked trout mousse into egg shaped quenelles and place around salad.

Note: very tasty light summer dish. Can be served as a main course or a tempting starter.

Pickled Herrings

Ingredients

5 herrings (cleaned, scaled, heads, tails and fins removed)
1 small onion (chopped)
1 bay leaf
1 sprig of parsley and 5 sprigs of dill
6 black peppercorns
250ml quality white wine vinegar
1 teaspoon of sea salt
250ml water

Method: place all the ingredients into a saucepan except dill and herring. Bring liquid to the boil and simmer for 1 minute. Leave to cool. Place a sprig of dill on the inside of each herring fillet and roll skin side out. Secure with a cocktail stick. Place in sterilised preserving jar, cover with liquid and secure lid. Leave for 2 days before using.

Note: a nice tossed salad with homemade brown bread accompanies this dish very well.

Artichokes and Cork Smoked Beef Salad

serves 4

Ingredients

A selection of salad leaves to serve 4
4 pre-prepared artichokes (roughly sliced)
150g Cork smoked beef (cut into very fine strips)
2 tablespoons of chives
Vinaigrette (see page 17)
Salt & milled black pepper

Method: place smoked beef, artichokes and chives into a bowl. Season with salt and milled black pepper and dress with vinaigrette. In a separate bowl, toss salad leaves with some vinaigrette.

To Assemble Dish: place salad leaves in the centre of a platter and place artichokes, smoked beef and chives around. Serve immediately.

Note: artichokes are available in the summer, so this makes an ideal salad with a difference.

A Parfait of Duck and Chicken Livers

serves 8 – 10 persons approx.

Ingredients

200g duck livers
200g chicken livers
1 teaspoon of cooking oil
300g melted butter
2 tablespoons of port
1 clove of garlic (finely chopped)
1 teaspoon of chopped thyme
Salt & milled black pepper

Method: season livers well and fry in hot oil. Add garlic and thyme and continue to cook until livers are just pink. Place livers in a food processor and gradually add melted butter and port. Pass through a sieve. Season to taste and pour into desired mould. Place in fridge to set.

Note: this terrine is excellent served with toasted brioche and homemade redcurrant jelly.

Beef and Tomato Sausage with a Potato Purée

Ingredients

4 beef and tomato sausages
50ml of cream
400g potato purée
1 tablespoon of cooking oil
1 onion (sliced)
1 knob of butter
2 streaky rashers (cut into lardons)
Seasoning to taste

Method: cook sausages in a hot pan with the cooking oil and set aside. Wipe pan clean, add butter and fry onions and bacon together until crispy. Reheat potato purée with butter and cream, and season to taste. Place potato purée onto a serving dish and neatly arrange sausage, bacon and onions around.

Note: in recent years there has been an increase in the number of butchers producing excellent quality sausages with a large variety of flavours available. The beef and tomato sausages are my favourite.

Pancakes Filled with Scrambled Eggs and accompanied by Clonakilty Black Pudding with a Cider Jus

serves 4

Ingredients

8 small pancakes
4 free range eggs
2 tablespoons of milk (for scrambled eggs)
50g butter
16 slices of black pudding
1 shallot (finely diced)
1 cooking apple
250ml cider
Salt & pepper to taste

Method: in a hot pan fry the black pudding with a little butter. Remove from the pan and set aside. Sweat shallot and apple in a little butter, add the cider and reduce to one-third of the original volume. Pass the sauce through a fine sieve and force the apple and shallot through with the back of a spoon. Return sauce to the boil. Correct seasoning, and whisk in remaining butter. Prepare scrambled eggs. (Be careful not to over-cook).

To Assemble Dish: place pancake in the centre of the plate and put a spoonful of scrambled egg on top of the pancake. Surround with 4 slices of black pudding. Place second pancake on top and pour cider jus around. Garnish with fresh herbs.

Note: this recipe seems to have the appearance of a dish you would serve for breakfast. By adding the pancake and the cider jus it makes an ideal starter or indeed can be served as a main course.

A Warm Smoked Haddock Salad

serves 4

Ingredients

500g smoked haddock
50ml virgin olive oil
Juice of $^1/_2$ lemon
2 tablespoons of dill (chopped)
Freshly milled black pepper
Assortment of crisp salad leaves
Vinaigrette dressing (see page 17)

Method: arrange finely sliced smoked haddock on a large plate. Mix olive oil and lemon juice and brush lightly on the smoked haddock. Sprinkle on dill and milled pepper and place under the grill or in the oven for 3-4 minutes. Toss salad leaves with the vinaigrette dressing. Place haddock in the centre of the plate and arrange salad leaves around the fish. Serve immediately.

Note: this is a very refreshing and delicious salad, particularly in the summer.

MAIN COURSES

Roast Wood Pigeon with an Elderberry Sauce

Ingredients

4 wood pigeons (pre prepared)
50g ripe elderberries
Juice of $^1/_2$ a lemon
1 clove of garlic
Sprig of thyme
1 shallot (roughly chopped)
150ml port
150ml water
25g butter
Oil for cooking
Salt & black milled pepper

Method: season the pigeons and put them into a hot pan with oil, add the garlic, shallot and thyme. Fry until lightly brown on both sides and then place in a hot oven and cook to desired point, preferably pink. Remove from the oven. Carefully remove the breasts and legs from the carcasses and set aside. Chop the bones, pour off all excess fat from the pan. Place the bones in the pan with the port, lemon juice and water, bring to the boil and skim. Add 35g of the elderberries, simmer gently for another 5 to 6 minutes, then pass through a fine sieve. Whisk in the butter and remaining elderberries and season to taste. Carve the pigeon breasts and arrange the legs neatly around four plates and pour on the sauce.

Fish Pie

Ingredients

500g mashed potatoes
2 egg yolks
Knob of butter
2 tablespoons of cream
2 tablespoons of chopped parsley
50g Irish Cheddar cheese (grated)
1 kilo assorted fish cut into cubes (i.e. cod, trout,
mussels [shelled], plaice)
100ml cream
50ml white wine
1/2 onion (finely diced)
1 teaspoon of lemon juice
100ml water
Seasoning to taste
25g Beurre Manié

Method: place water, wine, cream, onion and lemon
juice into a large saucepan. Bring to the boil, add fish
and return to the boil. Simmer for 1 minute, then remove fish and set aside. Reduce cooking juices slightly, whisk in Beurre Manié and simmer gently for a further 2 minutes. Place fish into large pie dish, then
pour on the sauce.

Potato Topping: place cream and butter in a saucepan,
add mashed potato and heat gently. Mix in the egg
yolk and parsley, and season to taste. Place this mixture on top of the fish in the pie dish and sprinkle with
grated Cheddar cheese. Place in a hot oven for 15 minutes. Then serve.

Roast Saddle of Rabbit with Mushrooms and an Armagnac Cream Sauce

serves 2

Ingredients

2 prepared saddle of rabbit
50g mushrooms (chopped)
1 shallot (chopped)
$1/2$ clove of garlic (chopped)
$1/2$ teaspoon thyme leaves (chopped)
2 teaspoons armagnac
2 tablespoons white wine
100ml cream
Knob of butter
2 tablespoons olive oil
Salt & milled black pepper

Method: season the rabbits and roast in a roasting tin with the olive oil. Place in the oven at 175° for 15 minutes approximately, ensuring to baste while it is cooking. Remove and set aside. Drain excess fat from the pan, add the chopped shallots, garlic and thyme. Then add the mushrooms with a knob of butter and toss until cooked. Add the armagnac and white wine, reduce slightly, then add the cream and reduce again to sauce consistency. Correct seasoning.

Prepare the saddle of rabbit by removing the 4 fillets from the bone. Slice the fillets and place back onto the bone. Then pour the sauce over and serve.

Hamburger of Prime Beef

serves 4

Ingredients

600g lean minced beef
1 tablespoon of Dijon mustard
2 medium shallots, finely diced
1 egg
1 tablespoon of parsley (chopped)
1 dash of Worcester sauce
Salt & pepper to taste

Method: combine all ingredients in a bowl and mix thoroughly. Shape neatly into 4 hamburgers each weighing 150g approximately. Pan-fry to desired point.

Note: a definite favourite with young and old. I would suggest serving the hamburgers with garlic croutons and braised red onions, and perhaps some sautéed potatoes.

Roast Chicken with Shallots, Bacon, Garlic and Mushrooms

serves 4

Ingredients

4 chicken breasts
50g butter
12 shallots
12 cloves of garlic
24 button mushrooms
2 tablespoons of cream
150ml chicken stock
50ml white wine
50g bacon (cut into lardons)
1 tablespoon of chopped parsley
200g potato purée
Salt & pepper to taste

Method: season chicken breasts and seal in a hot pan with a little butter until golden brown on each side. Remove and set aside. Add to the pan, shallots, bacon, garlic and mushrooms. Toss in butter until golden brown. Add wine and chicken stock to the pan and return the chicken breasts. Place in hot oven (170ºC approximately) for 10 to 15 minutes until chicken breasts are cooked. Reheat potato purée with cream and remaining butter. Season and add parsley.

To Assemble Dish: place potato purée in the centre of a dish. Neatly arrange the chicken breasts and remaining ingredients around. Pour the sauce over the breasts of chicken.

Baked Cod with Courgettes and Parmesan Cheese

serves 4

Ingredients

600g fresh cod
1 courgette
50g fresh Parmesan cheese, grated
1 ripe tomato peeled (de-seeded and chopped)
A little olive oil
Knob of butter
Lemon juice for flavour
Salt & pepper to taste

Method: cut cod into 4 pieces, 150g each. Season with salt, pepper, and lemon juice, and brush with olive oil. Slice courgettes thinly and blanch for 2 minutes. Arrange courgette slices neatly on top of the fresh cod pieces. Place some chopped tomato in the centre of each piece and sprinkle with Parmesan cheese. Place on a buttered baking tray. Cook in a moderate oven for 15 minutes (approximately). When cooked, remove and serve.

Note: this dish can be served with its natural cooking juices, which can be enhanced with a little butter, cream and fresh herbs.

Grilled Pork Chops with an Apple and Onion Compôte

Ingredients

4 pork chops
1 apple
1 onion
Knob of butter
$1/2$ clove of garlic
$1/2$ teaspoon of thyme leaves
Olive oil for cooking
Salt & milled black pepper

Method: dry pork chops well with kitchen paper and brush with olive oil. Season and place on a hot grill pan and sear until well marked on both sides. When cooked, set aside. Melt the butter in a saucepan and slowly cook the onion, apple, garlic and thyme. Season with milled pepper and salt. Arrange chops and Compôte on a serving dish.

Note: when buying the chops, ask your butcher for well hung pork. The reason for this is that the pork chops are tender and more flavoursome.

44

Smoked Haddock on a Bed of Irish Potatoes with a Light Parsley Cream Sauce

Ingredients

600g smoked haddock
1 shallot (chopped)
30ml white wine
250ml fresh cream
2 tablespoons of fresh parsley
30ml of fish stock

Purée Ingredients

4 large potatoes
50g butter
seasoning

Method: prepare haddock and cut into 4 even sized pieces. Poach in cream, white wine, stock and shallot. When cooked, remove and set aside. Reduce liquid to sauce consistency. Pass through a fine sieve. Correct seasoning and add chopped parsley. Boil potatoes until cooked and drain water off. Purée the potatoes. Add butter and season to taste.

To Assemble Dish: place purée on a platter and place haddock neatly on top. Pour parsley sauce around.

Casserole of Beef and Stout

Ingredients

750g stewing beef
250ml stout
1.25 litres brown stock
1 medium onion (chopped)
1 bunch of tied herbs
1 carrot
1 stick of celery (chopped)
2 tablespoons of vegetable oil
1 clove of garlic
30g Beurre Manié
Salt & milled black pepper
1 tablespoon chopped parsley (for garnish)
1 knob of butter

Method: brown the beef in a very hot pan with the oil. Heat a medium sized saucepan with the butter, add vegetables and cook for 1 minute approximately. Add the beef, stock, tied herbs and stout. Bring to the boil, skim and simmer for 1 hour until meat is tender. Correct seasoning and whisk in Beurre Manié to thicken. Before serving, add the chopped parsley.

Baked Meatballs with Pasta Topped with Irish Cheddar Cheese Sauce

serves 4

Meatballs – Ingredients

500g lean minced beef
1 tablespoon Dijon mustard
2 medium shallots (finely diced)
1 egg
1 tablespoon mixed herbs (chopped)
1 dash of Worcester sauce
Salt & milled black pepper to taste
Cooking oil
Flour for coating

Method: combine all ingredients in a bowl and shape into sixteen meatballs, each weighing 30g approximately. Season, coat with flour and brown in hot oil. Place on a roasting tray and cook in the oven for 15 minutes. Remove meatballs and drain off all fat. Set aside.

Tomato Sauce – Ingredients

4 tomatoes (peeled, de-seeded and diced)
2 cloves of garlic
100ml tomato juice
1 shallot, finely diced
1/2 teaspoon chopped thyme
25ml white wine
1 knob of butter

Method: sweat shallot, garlic and thyme in the butter until soft. Add the white wine and reduce slightly. Add the tomato and tomato juice and cook for a further minute. Season to taste and correct consistency.

Cheese Sauce – Ingredients

200ml milk
100ml cream
30g Beurre Manié
30g Irish Cheddar cheese
Salt & milled black pepper

Method: boil the milk and cream and whisk in the Beurre Manié to thicken. Cook for 4 to 5 minutes. Whisk in cheese and season to taste.

Pasta Dough – Ingredients

100g pasta dough (or alternatively use good quality lasagna sheets)

Method: roll out thinly and cut into two sheets to match the shape of your serving dish. Blanch for 2 to 3 minutes.

Topping – Ingredients

20g white breadcrumbs
20g grated Cheddar cheese

To Assemble Dish: line the pie dish with some of the cheese sauce. Place a layer of pasta on top, arrange meatballs on top of pasta and pour on the tomato sauce. Place the second sheet of pasta on top and pour on the remaining cheese sauce. Sprinkle on cheese and breadcrumbs and place in a hot oven for 15 minutes.

Moussaka

Ingredients

800g lean mince
1 small onion (finely diced)
2 cloves of garlic (crushed)
1 tablespoon mixed herbs (chopped) [i.e. thyme,
tarragon, parsley]
1 tablespoon tomato purée
100g plum tomatoes (chopped)
150ml white wine
1 teaspoon flour
Salt & milled black pepper
4 medium potatoes (par cooked)
1 aubergine (sliced)
Olive oil and butter for cooking

Sauce

150ml milk
150ml cream
25g Beurre Manié
50g grated Cheddar cheese
$1/2$ teaspoon of mixed spice

Method: boil milk and cream and whisk in Beurre
Manié. Cook for 2 to 3 minutes, stirring continuously.
Whisk in grated Cheddar cheese and mixed spice.

Mince: fry the mince in very hot oil with the onion,
garlic and herbs. Cook for 5 minutes. Drain off the fat.
Add tomato purée and flour, then add white wine and
plum tomatoes.

Cook for a further 8 to 10 minutes. Slice the potatoes and aubergines thinly and fry them separately in
hot oil until cooked.

To Assemble Dish: in a pie dish, place alternate layers
of potatoes, mince meat and aubergines and finally top
with sauce.

49

Roast Pheasant with a Chestnut and Lemon Stuffing

serves 2

Ingredients

1 pheasant
50g mixed vegetables roughly chopped (carrots, onions and celery)
Sprig of thyme
Oil for cooking

Stuffing

150g breadcrumbs
50g chestnuts (cooked, peeled and roughly chopped)
30g butter
2 shallots finely diced
Juice of 1 lemon
Grated ring of 1 lemon
1 tablespoon of mixed herbs (chopped)
Salt & milled black pepper

Method: wash the pheasant well. Dry, season and set aside.

To Make Stuffing and to Cook Pheasant: melt the butter in a medium sized saucepan. Add the shallots and mixed herbs and cook until soft. Mix in remaining ingredients and season to taste. Fill the pheasant carcass with the stuffing and seal the opening with some twine or thread.

Place the pheasant on a roasting tray surrounded with the vegetables and some cooking oil. Place in a hot oven (180°C) and cook for 1 hour approximately, depending on size. Carve and serve with some bread sauce (see page 16).

Clifford's Gourmet Irish Stew

Ingredients

1 1/2 litres water approximately
1 leg of lamb (ask the butcher to bone the joint and to chop the bones into small pieces)
2 large carrots
1 large onion (chopped)
1 small white turnip (chopped)
4 potatoes (chopped)
1 stick of celery (chopped)
50g green cabbage (finely shredded and lightly cooked)
1 leek (finely sliced)
100ml cream
Dash of Worcester sauce
Chopped parsley
2 tablespoons of raw pearl barley (soaked and cooked)
Pinch of sea salt and black pepper
Bunch of thyme

Method: cut the lamb into cubes and put in a large pot. Cover with cold water. Bring to the boil. Drain and rinse the lamb, then replace in a clean pot. Add the bones to the pot with thyme, black pepper and salt. Cover with 1 1/2 litres of cold water. Next add the vegetables but keep aside 1 carrot, the white turnip, 2 potatoes and the green cabbage for later use as a garnish. Cover the pot and cook for approximately 1 hour or until the meat is tender. Remove the meat bones from the pot and discard. Liquidise the cooked vegetables and the liquid. Return to the pot. Add pearl barley, cream and Worcester sauce. Add chopped parsley.

Neatly chop and blanch the remaining vegetables. Return the meat and blanched vegetables to the pot. Taste for seasoning. Garnish the stew with cooked shredded cabbage.

Note: this is a modernised version of a traditional recipe and had proved very successful on our menus.

VEGETABLES AND VEGETARIAN

Deep Fried Cauliflower with a Tomato and Garlic Sauce

serves 4

Ingredients

12 cauliflower florets (par cooked)
Salt & milled black pepper
Flour for dusting
Chopped chives for garnish

Batter

500ml water
1 egg yolk
100g cornflour
100g plain flour
$1/4$ teaspoon baking powder

Method: combine water and egg yolk and mix well. Gradually add flour, cornflour and baking powder. Place in fridge and chill.

Tomato and Garlic Sauce

4 tomatoes (peeled, de-seeded and diced)
2 cloves of garlic (peeled and crushed)
100ml tomato juice
1 shallot (finely diced)
$1/2$ teaspoon chopped thyme
25ml white wine
1 knob of butter

Method: sweat shallot, garlic and thyme in the butter until soft. Add white wine and reduce slightly. Add tomato and tomato juice and cook for a further minute. Season to taste and correct consistency.

To Cook Cauliflower: dry cauliflower well and season with salt and pepper. Coat lightly with flour and dip into batter. Remove and shake off excess batter. Deep fry in hot oil (180°C approximately) until golden brown.

To Assemble Dish: place 3 florets on each plate and pour sauce around. Garnish with chopped chives.

Chetwynd Blue Cheese Dip

Ingredients

4 tablespoons of natural yoghurt
100g blue cheese
150ml fresh cream
Juice of $1/2$ lemon
1 tablespoon chopped chives
Salt & milled black pepper to taste

Method: blend cheese and yoghurt in food processor. Remove and set aside. Lightly whip cream, add to yoghurt and cheese mixture, add lemon juice and chives. Correct seasoning.

Note: serve chilled. Makes an ideal dip for crackers or crudites. The blue cheese dip can also be served with smoked fish salad.

Cabbage with Raisins and Nuts

serves 4 – 6

Ingredients

2 heads of young tender cabbage
25g chopped cashew nuts (toasted)
25g raisins
Knob of butter
1/2 onion (sliced)
Seasoning to taste

Method: wash the cabbage and cut into strips. Plunge into a saucepan of boiling water, with a pinch of salt. Bring to the boil and simmer for 10 minutes, and drain well.

Place the knob of butter into a pan, add the onion and cook until soft. Add the cabbage, raisins and nuts. Season to taste and serve.

Notes: this is an ideal vegetarian dish using cabbage in a modern way. Crispy, crunchy and very tasty.

Fried Potato Cake with Cork Spiced Beef

Ingredients

1 large baking potato
50g cooked spiced beef (cut into fine strips)
1 tablespoon chopped mixed herbs (parsley, chives and chervil)
Olive oil for cooking
Knob of butter
Pinch of mixed spice
Salt & milled black pepper

Method: wash and peel the potato, slice thinly and cut into matchstick size. Place into a bowl with the spiced beef, herbs and mixed spice. Season with salt and milled pepper.

Heat a large metal frying pan, pour in the olive oil, and add the knob of butter and the potato mixture. Press firmly down with a palate knife and cook on a high heat until golden brown. Carefully turn over and cook on the other side until golden brown. They are now ready to be served.

Open Tomato Tartlet

Ingredients

100g puff pastry (thinly rolled out)
1 teaspoon of Dijon mustard
1 large onion (sliced)
4 large ripe Irish tomatoes
Sprig of chopped basil
50g Irish Cheddar cheese (grated)
Salt and milled pepper to taste
1 knob of butter
Pinch of salt

Method: roll out pastry very thinly and line 4 individual tartlet dishes. Pierce the base with a fork. (This is to prevent rising of the pastry). Lightly brush the base with the mustard and place in the fridge to rest. In a hot pan, sauté the onion until transparent in colour. Place a layer of cooked onion on each tartlet and season to taste. Sprinkle the grated cheese on each tartlet and add sliced tomatoes. Now sprinkle with basil and a little sugar to counteract the acidity of the tomatoes. Bake in a medium oven (150° approximately) until cooked. (Ensure that pastry is cooked properly.) Serve hot or cold with a selection of salad leaves.

Spinach Pancakes with a Stir-Fry of Bean Sprouts

serves 4

Ingredients

Pancake Batter (makes 10 pancakes)

500ml milk
50g melted butter
200g flour
2 eggs
75g cooked spinach (finely chopped)

Method: place milk, flour and egg in a bowl and whisk until smooth. Pour on melted butter and add cooked spinach and season to taste. Set aside in fridge for 1 hour. Prepare pancakes by adding the batter mixture to a hot pan with a little oil. Cook pancakes on each side until golden brown. Keep warm.

Stir-Fry Ingredients

300g bean sprouts
1 large onion (sliced)
150g mushrooms (sliced)
2 tablespoons of Sunflower oil
2 tablespoons of Soya sauce
1 teaspoon of finely chopped root ginger
1 teaspoon of coriander
Seasoning to taste

Method: heat oil in large pan or wok until very hot. Add onions and ginger and toss quickly. Add mushrooms and bean sprouts and cook for a further 1 or 2 minutes. Then add seasoning and coriander, finishing by adding the Soya sauce.

Ensure that all vegetables are cooked but still crunchy.

To assemble dish: divide stir-fry between four pancakes, fold over and serve.

Note: there are a number of oils on the market. Sesame Seed oil is excellent with stir-frys but again, it is a matter of taste whichever you choose.

Fried Potato Pancakes

Ingredients

500g potato purée
150g flour
5 eggs
300ml cream
Salt
1 tablespoon of chopped parsley
50g chopped bacon (fried)
Oil for cooking

Method: combine all ingredients together and rest in fridge for 1 hour. Heat a small omelette pan and pour some of the mixture into the pan. Cook until golden brown. Turn, and again cook until golden brown. Repeat until mixture is finished.

Braised Lettuce Filled with Mushrooms

serves 4

Ingredients

2 heads of lettuce
150g button mushrooms (sliced)
1 cooking apple (peeled and diced)
$^1/_2$ clove of garlic (chopped)
1 shallot (chopped)
15g of streaky rasher (cooked and chopped)
100ml chicken stock
1 knob of butter
Seasoning to taste

Method: blanch the lettuce in salted water for 1 minute. Refresh in cold water and set aside. Fry the garlic and shallot in a knob of butter, and add the mushrooms and apple. Season to taste. When cooked, place in a food processor and purée. Mix in the rasher, remove and set a side.

Prepare the lettuce by removing the core and cut it into quarters. Place the mushroom filling in the centre of each quarter and fold over neatly to form parcels. Place in a casserole dish and pour on the hot stock. Place in a hot oven for 10 to 12 minutes.

Note: this is an interesting way of using lettuce and this dish is particularly tasty.

Braised Red Onions

serves 4

Ingredients

200g red onions
1 tablespoon of honey
1 knob of butter
20ml red wine vinegar
30ml red wine
$1/2$ teaspoon of thyme leaves, chopped
Salt and pepper to taste

Method: place onions and butter in an ovenproof pan and sweat until soft. Add honey and caramelise. Add vinegar, wine and thyme. Season to taste and place in a hot oven for 8-10 minutes until juices are absorbed.

Note: a very versatile vegetable, very nice served with game or any red meat.

Avocado Sorbet

yields 1 litre approx.

Ingredients

5 ripe avocados (peeled and stones removed)
850ml water
225g sugar
Juice of 2 lemons
1 egg white

Method: make a stock syrup by combining the sugar and water. Boil until sugar has dissolved. Allow to cool before using. Purée avocado flesh with lemon juice in a food processor and add to the chilled stock syrup. Pour mixture into the ice-cream machine and churn for 15 minutes. Add egg white and continue to cool for another 15 minutes according to the cooling power of your machine. Place sorbet into frosted glass bowls and serve.

New Irish Potatoes Flavoured with Fresh Mint

Ingredients

500g new potatoes
Knob of butter
Fresh mint leaves
Salt and pepper to taste

Method: wash potatoes and place in boiling water with a pinch of salt and some fresh mint. Simmer until cooked (approximately 20 minutes). When cooked, brush with butter and sprinkle with fresh mint leaves and serve immediately.

Prune and Apple Stuffing

yields 500g approx.

Ingredients

25g butter
1-2 large shallots (finely diced)
1 clove of garlic (crushed)
1 tablespoon of chopped herbs (parsley and chives)
Juice of $^1/_2$ a lemon
Pinch of nutmeg
Salt and pepper
100g breadcrumbs
150g prunes (chopped)
1 large apple (grated)

Method: melt the butter and add the shallots and garlic. Cook until soft but not coloured. Add the herbs and lemon juice. Season with nutmeg, salt and pepper. Combine this mixture with the breadcrumbs. Mix in the prunes and apple. Taste, and correct seasoning if necessary.

Note: this stuffing goes particularly well with a loin of pork.

DESSERTS

Spicy Apple and Raisin Flan

10 portions approx.

Ingredients

500g sugar pastry
10 medium sized cooking apples
150g raisins
$^1/_2$ teaspoon ground cinnamon
$^1/_2$ teaspoon lemon juice
1 teaspoon dark brown sugar
25g icing sugar
50g butter

Method: roll out pastry and line flan ring (20.5cm). Pierce base with fork, cook blind and set aside. Peel 8 of the apples and roughly chop. Put the butter, apples, brown sugar, lemon juice and spices into a saucepan. Sweat for 2 to 3 minutes, add raisins and cook for a further minute.

Pour this mixture into a flan ring. Peel the remaining 2 apples, half and thinly slice, arrange neatly in a fan shape around the top of the flan. Sprinkle with icing sugar and glaze under the grill until golden brown.

Note: serve this flan with freshly whipped cream.

Meringue and Hazelnut Parfait

serves 6 – 8 Persons

Ingredients

50g hazelnuts
150ml cream
4 egg whites
125g icing sugar
30ml Irish Mist
Toasted chopped hazelnuts and icing sugar to decorate

Method: line a 20.5cm cake tin with cling film. Toast the hazelnuts, cool and grind to a course powder. Lightly whip the cream. Whisk the egg whites until stiff. Gradually whisk in the sieved sugar. Fold in the nuts, cream and Irish Mist. Spoon into the cake tin and freeze for at least 4 hours or overnight.

When ready, sprinkle with hazelnuts and dust with icing sugar. Pour a little Irish Mist around if you wish.

Note: this dessert can be made by using individual moulds rather then the cake tin version.

Poached Plums in Red Wine Scented with Cinnamon and Ginger

serves 2

Ingredients

8 plums
300ml red wine
1 tablespoon of Irish honey
2 tablespoons of brown sugar
Pinch of cinnamon
1 teaspoon of finely chopped root ginger
Juice of 1 lemon
Juice of 1 orange
2 teaspoons of arrowroot

Method: combine all ingredients together except plums and arrowroot and simmer for 2 minutes. Dissolve the arrowroot in a little water and add to the sauce to thicken.

Prepare plums by cutting into segments, then add to the sauce and cook for a further minute. Serve hot.

Note: this dessert is particularly nice served with a vanilla ice-cream.

Compôte of Bananas in a Light Lime Syrup

serves 4

Ingredients

6 bananas
1 lime
100g sugar
250ml water

Method: place sugar and water plus the lime juice into a saucepan. Grate small amount of lime zest and add into syrup. Bring to the boil and simmer for 2 minutes. Slice bananas, place in serving dish and pour syrup over.

Note: this is a very simple dessert which can be produced in minutes. It is very refreshing and makes a nice light dessert.

Baby Meringues Scented with Irish Mist

Ingredients

50g egg whites
100g caster sugar
1 tablespoon of Irish Mist

Method: using a clean bowl and whisk, beat egg whites until they reach a stiff peak. Continue whisking and add two-thirds of the sugar. Continue whisking until the meringue is very stiff. Fold in remaining sugar with a spatula. Finally fold in Irish Mist. With a piping bag and star nozzle, pipe onto greaseproof paper to desired shape and place in oven to cook for 1 hour at 100°C.

Note: this is a good way to use up egg whites. The baby meringues can be served with afternoon tea or coffee.

Caramelised Pancake filled with Bananas

serves 8

Ingredients

8 pre-cooked pancakes
8 bananas
125ml whipped cream
Pastry cream
Icing sugar for dusting
Caramel sauce

Caramel Sauce Ingredients

250g sugar
150ml water
150ml cream
100g unsalted butter

Pastry Cream Ingredients

250ml milk
3 egg yolks
50g caster sugar
2 – 3 drops of vanilla essence
50g plain flour

Method:
Caramel Sauce: boil sugar and water in a saucepan until sugar is dissolved. Allow to caramelise until nut brown in colour. Remove from heat and whisk in cream and butter. Set aside for later use.

Pastry Cream: boil milk and add vanilla. Set aside. Cream yolks and sugar. Add flour. Mix well. Add a little of the milk. Then pour on remaining milk. Return to heat and cook out. Allow to cool.

To Assemble dish: heat pancakes and place on plates. Reheat caramel sauce and add sliced bananas. Remove from heat. Fold in whipped cream to the pastry cream. Place a spoonful of pastry cream in the centre of the pancake on each plate. Pour caramel and banana mixture neatly around the plate. Fold pancake over and dust with icing sugar.

BREADS

Wholemeal Yeast Pancakes

yields 5–6 pancakes

Ingredients

50g each of wholemeal and white plain flour
5g fresh yeast
150ml warm milk
15ml oil
2 egg whites
¹/₂ teaspoon of salt
¹/₂ teaspoon of sugar

Method: dissolve the yeast in the warm milk. Combine the 2 flours, sugar and salt. Mix together the milk and the flour mixtures and place in a large bowl. Cover with cling film and allow to ferment for 1 hour. Whisk and fold in egg whites to the mixture. Heat a non stick frying pan, and add some oil. Pour about 30ml of batter into the pan and fry until the mixture bubbles and the underside is golden. Flip over and fry the other side. Place on a tea towel, cover and keep warm while you are cooking the rest.

Note: these pancakes can be cooked in advance and preheated at the last minute. The pancakes are very good served with smoked fish.

Another alternative is to serve them with home-made jam.

Tomato, Olive and Garlic Bread

yields 3 French sticks

Ingredients

500g bakers flour
300ml water
15g fresh yeast
1 tablespoon of salt
100g sun dried tomatoes (cut into strips)
100g black olives (stones removed and sliced)
3 cloves of garlic (crushed)
$^{1}/_{2}$ small onion, very finely sliced
Salt & milled black pepper
1 teaspoon of olive oil
Egg wash

Method: dissolve yeast in a little of the warm water. Sieve the flour and salt into a mixing bowl, add dissolved yeast and remaining water. Beat with dough hook for a few minutes. Place in a bowl and cover with a damp cloth. Leave to prove for 40 minutes approximately until it doubles in size. Knead your dough and divide into 3 even sized French sticks. Brush with egg wash and leave to prove in a warm area for 10 minutes. Meanwhile, fry the onion and garlic in the olive oil and mix in the olives and sundried tomatoes. Season with salt and pepper. Make an incision in the centre of each French stick and place the filling through the centre. Place in oven at 175°C for 20 minutes.

Note: it is advisable to place a tray of water in the bottom of your oven to create a moist heat for baking your French sticks.

Tea Brack

yields 1 loaf

Ingredients

200g wholemeal flour
150g raisins
1 egg
1 egg yolk
150g brown sugar
125ml strong, cold tea
25ml Irish whiskey
1 tablespoon of honey for glazing
1 teaspoon of baking powder
Pinch of salt

Method: combine all ingredients in a mixing bowl except for the honey. Mix well and pour into a greased loaf tin (base lined with grease proof paper). Bake at 165°C for 45 minutes. When cooked, brush the top with warm honey to give it a nice glaze.

Brown Soda Bread

yields 1 loaf

Ingredients

250g wholemeal flour
150g plain flour
25g brown sugar
1 teaspoon of salt
1 teaspoon of bread soda
1 egg
25g butter
250ml buttermilk

Method: sieve plain flour, bread soda and salt into a bowl. Add wholemeal flour and sugar and mix. Melt butter and add to mixture. Add buttermilk and egg. Mix well and shape into a cake. Cook at 165°C for 45 minutes.

Michael's White Scones

Ingredients

225g white flour
150ml buttermilk
2 eggs (beaten)
50g butter
15g baking powder
50g caster sugar
Pinch of salt

Method: rub the butter into the flour. Add salt, sugar and baking powder. Add half a beaten egg and then mix in the buttermilk to form a smooth dough. Roll out to 2.5 cm of thickness. Using a 5 cm diameter cutter and cut into scone shape. Brush with remaining beaten egg and cook for 15 – 20 minutes at 145ºC.

PRESERVES

Gooseberry Jam

Ingredients

500g gooseberries
500g sugar
250ml water

Method: wash the gooseberries and top and tail. Place the gooseberries and water into a large saucepan. Bring to the boil and simmer until the gooseberries are tender. Add the sugar and boil rapidly until setting point is reached.

Note: a few points about jam making in general.

You cannot go wrong with jam if the sugar is heated to facilitate dissolving. Pots are warmed to sterilise.

Frequent stirring, particularly towards the end of boiling also helps in jam making.

Rub a little butter around the inside of the pot before starting. It makes a big difference as this prevents sticking.

Michael's Homemade Lemonade

yields 1 litre approx.

Ingredients

Juice of 4 lemons
Grated zest of one lemon
2 strips of cucumber peelings
6 leaves of fresh mint
1 litre of boiling water
100g sugar

Method: combine all ingredients and allow to cool. Place in fridge to chill for approximately 2 hours, then strain through a fine sieve. Serve chilled with slices of lemon and crushed ice.

Note: this is best served on a hot and humid day. It is a most refreshing drink and will quench any thirst!

Strawberry Jam

Ingredients

3 kilo fresh strawberries
2.5 kilo sugar
Juice of 2 lemons

Method: hull and wash the strawberries. Place in a large saucepan with the lemon juice. Bring to boiling point and simmer until reduced slightly. Stir as often as you can as strawberry jam has no water added. Add warm sugar and bring to the boil. Boil for 20 minutes approximately or until setting point is reached. Place jam in sterilised jars and fill to the top with jam. Allow to cool before placing greaseproof paper on top. Seal, date and label.

Note: this is the recipe I use all the time. The lemon juice acts as pectin for the strawberries and still the fruit has a nice fresh flavour as cooking time is less.

Cranberry and Orange Compôte

Ingredients

800g cranberries
500ml water
4 oranges
200g sugar

Method: peel and segment the oranges. Chop the segments and set aside. Squeeze the juice out of the pulp into a clean saucepan. Wash the cranberries well and add to the saucepan. Add the sugar and cover with the water. Bring to the boil and skim. Simmer gently for 45 minutes approximately. Add the chopped orange segments towards the end of cooking.

Note: this makes an ideal accompaniment for game or fowl. When cooking cranberries it is important to remember that only tin lined copper or stainless steel pots should be used. Aluminium or iron pots may cause discoloration.

GLOSSARY

Baste

To moisten food with its own juices during cooking ie roast meats, poultry and game.

Beurre Manié

A mixture of butter and flour used for thickening sauces or soups.

Blanched

Vegetables brought to the boil, then refreshed in cold water.

Braise

Culinary term for cooking in the oven with a covered lid.

Bunch of Tied Herbs

A neat bundle of herbs used to flavour foods during cooking otherwise known as bouquet garni.

Compôte

Culinary term for stewed fruit.

Cook Blind

Term used when cooking pastry flan where the flan is cooked with greaseproof paper and pulses are on top to prevent pastry from rising.

Lardons

Pieces of streaky bacon cut into strips and fried.

Parboiled

Partly cooked in salted boiling water.

Purée

Pulp foods.

Quenelles

Mousse or purée of meat, fish or vegetables moulded into oval pieces.

Reduce

Term used when reducing stocks or sauces to achieve the desired consistency.

Sabayon

Yolks of eggs and a little liquid cooked until creamy.

Setting Point

A term used for jams and preserves. To ascertain if the jam is sufficiently boiled, put a spoonful on a plate and leave it in a cold place. If a thin skin forms over it or if the jam sets, it is ready.

Skim

To remove scum from stocks, sauces, soups and jams during cooking.

Sweat

To cook in butter or oil without colouring.

CONVERSION TABLES

To change ounces to grams multiply by 28.35
To change pounds to kilograms multiply by .47
To change pints to litres multiply by .24
To change teaspoons to millilitres multiply by 5
To change tablespoons to millilitres multiply by 15
For example:

Metric	Imperial	American
15g	$\frac{1}{2}$ ounce	1 tablespoon
100g	4 ounces	$\frac{1}{2}$ cup
225g	8 ounces	1 cup
50ml	2 fl ounces	$\frac{1}{2}$ cup
100ml	4 fl ounces	$\frac{1}{2}$ cup
225ml	8 fl ounces	1 cup
600ml	20 fl ounces [1 pint]	2 $\frac{1}{2}$ cups

Equivalent weights and measures

3 teaspoons	1 tablespoon [$1\frac{1}{2}$ fl oz]
4 tablespoons	$\frac{1}{4}$ cup [2 fl oz]
16 tablespoons	1 cup
1 cup	8 fl ounces

Temperatures

Low 110–160 degrees C	225–350 degrees F
Moderate 180–200C	530–400 F
Hot 220–230 C	425–450 F
Very Hot 250 C	500 F

NOTES